Spe

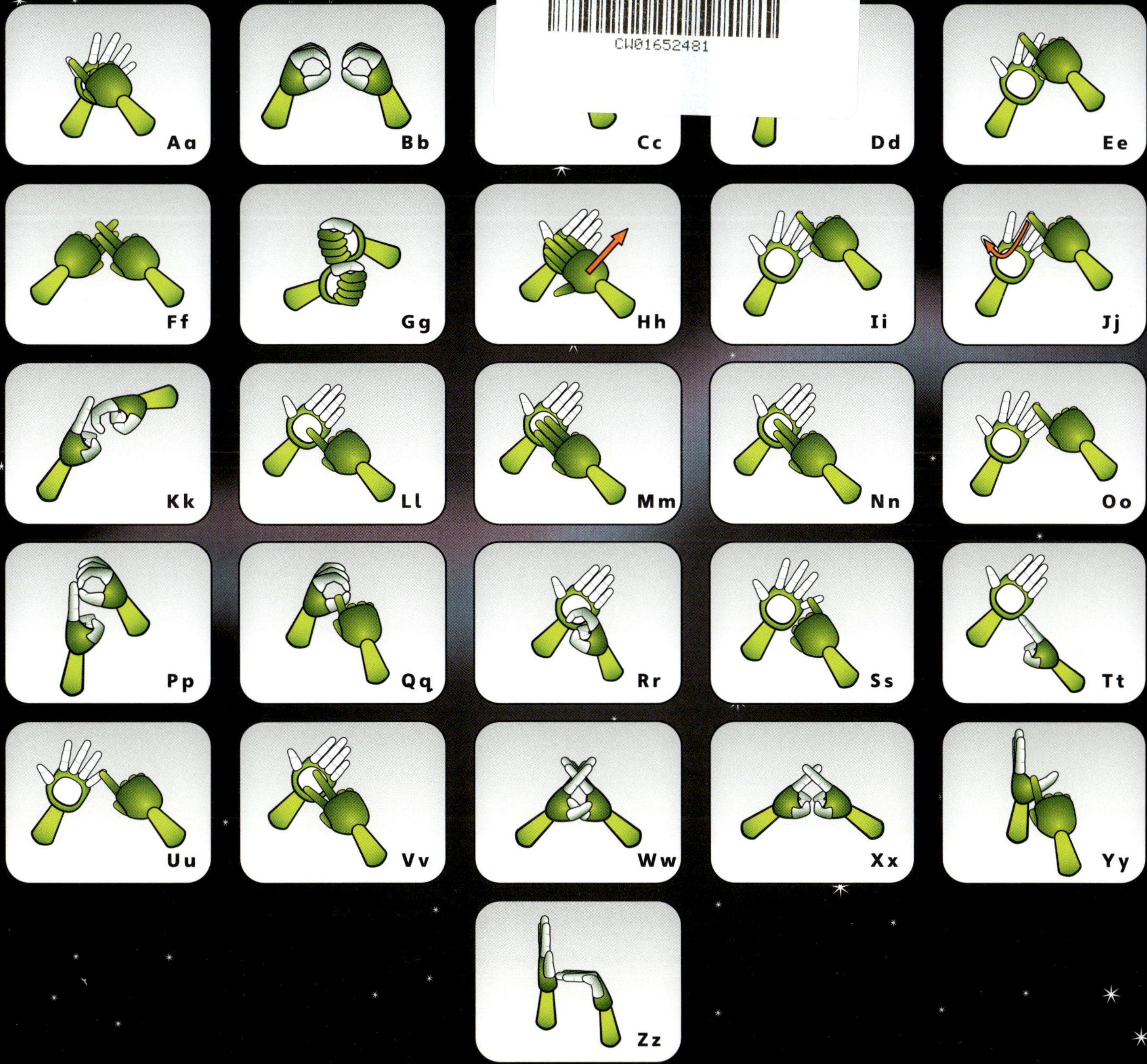

Aa
Bb
Cc
Dd
Ee
Ff
Gg
Hh
Ii
Jj
Kk
Ll
Mm
Nn
Oo
Pp
Qq
Rr
Ss
Tt
Uu
Vv
Ww
Xx
Yy
Zz

Zip

Zip is a friendly space alien from planet Zee. He loves to learn. Zip uses his hands to speak to his friends. He can't wait to teach the people of planet Earth all about sign language. Zip is the captain of his spaceship.

Pella

Pella is Zip's best friend. She also comes from planet Zee. Pella is very brave. Although she is a little younger than Zip and Statz, she isn't afraid of anything and is always the first of the three friends to try new things.

Statz

Statz is in charge of computers on the spaceship. He loves gadgets. Statz uses his Zablet to help him and his friends out of sticky situations. He is excited to learn about planet Earth and all the people who live here.

Goober

Goober is an unexpected guest on the friends' adventures. A greedy and naughty space stowaway, Goober has the ability to change his colour and shape so is always jumping out and surprising Zip, Pella and Statz.

Zip's top tips

Zip and friends are here to help you talk in a fun new way - spell with your fingers and talk with your hands. Follow these top tips to get the most from their adventures:

- **Share the book together and enjoy the story**
- **Play with the signs**
- **Use Zip's alphabet to make your own words**
- **Visit Space School, enjoy the activities and have fun**
- **Watch out for Goober...**

SignSpell

Zip and the Journey Home

The friends are in the control room of the spaceship. A light flashes on the panel to tell them they have an incoming message.

"It's a message from home," says Zip. His friends join him to watch.

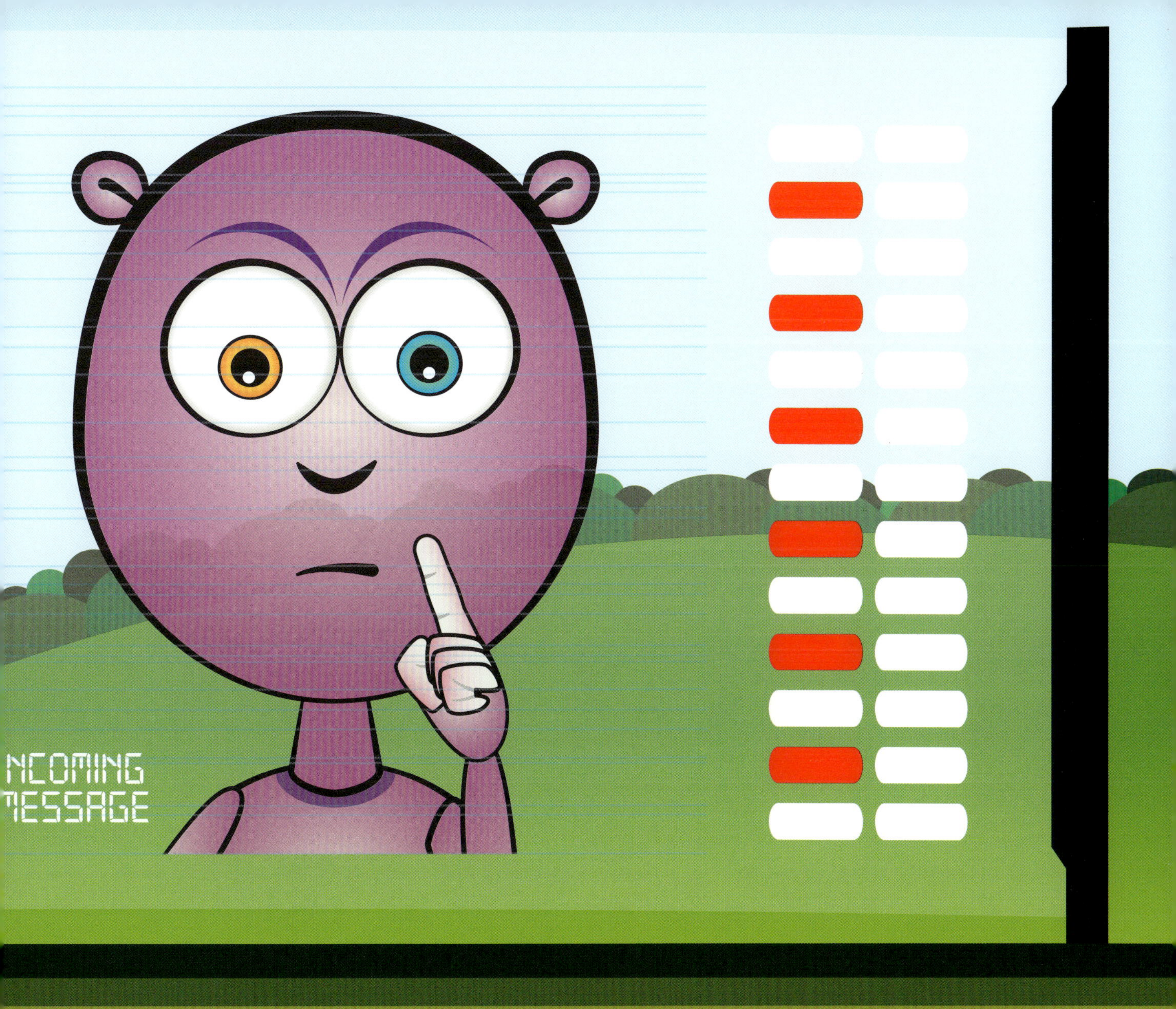

An alien appears on the screen and tells them they have to return to planet Zee straight away.

“He looked quite cross,” says Pella. “I wonder what the problem is?”

“It doesn’t matter,” says Zip. “We have to go home. Prepare the spaceship for take-off.”

Happy
x2
Album
11:36
CRAZY KINGDOM

Pella thinks about home and it makes her feel happy. "I've missed Zilli, my pet zyloplop," she says.

As Pella daydreams about her pet, she leans on Zip's seat. Her elbow presses a button and his chair is suddenly launched out of a hatch in the spaceship.

Zip is sure he will dislike this adventure.

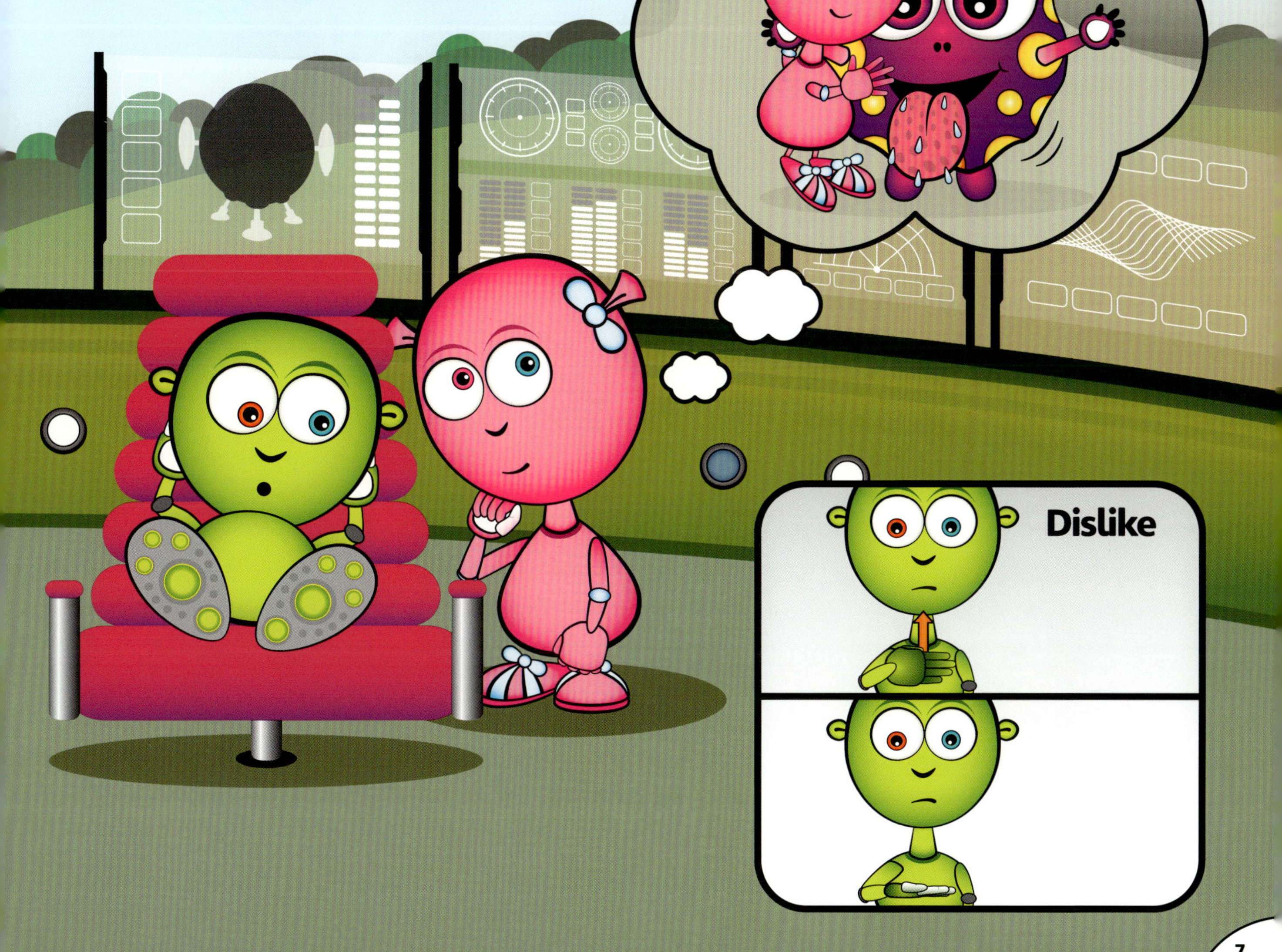

Zip shoots through the air at lightning speed. He is scared as the climbs higher and higher in the sky.

When the chair slows and starts to fall back to the ground, a parachute opens. He starts to feel calm again.

Calm

As the chair floats back down, Zip can see for miles and miles around. He thinks about how much he will miss planet Earth.

Statz and Pella are waiting outside the spaceship to make sure he lands safely. “I’m so sorry, Zip,” says Pella. “I’m glad you’re OK.”

Zip, Pella and Statz make their way back to the spaceship.

From outside Zip can see just how dirty the spaceship is. “We can’t take the ship home like this,” says Zip. “I would be embarrassed.”

Statz takes out his Zablet. “I have an idea,” he says. “Humans clean their vehicles at a place called the car wash. Let’s go there.”

Embarrassed

The friends take the spaceship to a nearby car wash.
The machine is just big enough for it to fit through.

Zip steers into the car wash and they wait to see what happens next.

They jerk forwards and little bubbles begin to appear all over the windows. Soon all they can see are giant soapy bubbles. Zip, Pella and Statz like watching the bubbles pop all around them.

Space School

Take a look at the pictures from the story.
See if you can spell each one using Zip's alphabet.

Out of the car wash the spaceship looks clean and sparkly. It is so shiny that Zip, Pella and Statz have to put on their sunglasses to take a proper look.

"Wow!" says Zip. "This is a spaceship to be proud of. I think we are ready for take-off now."

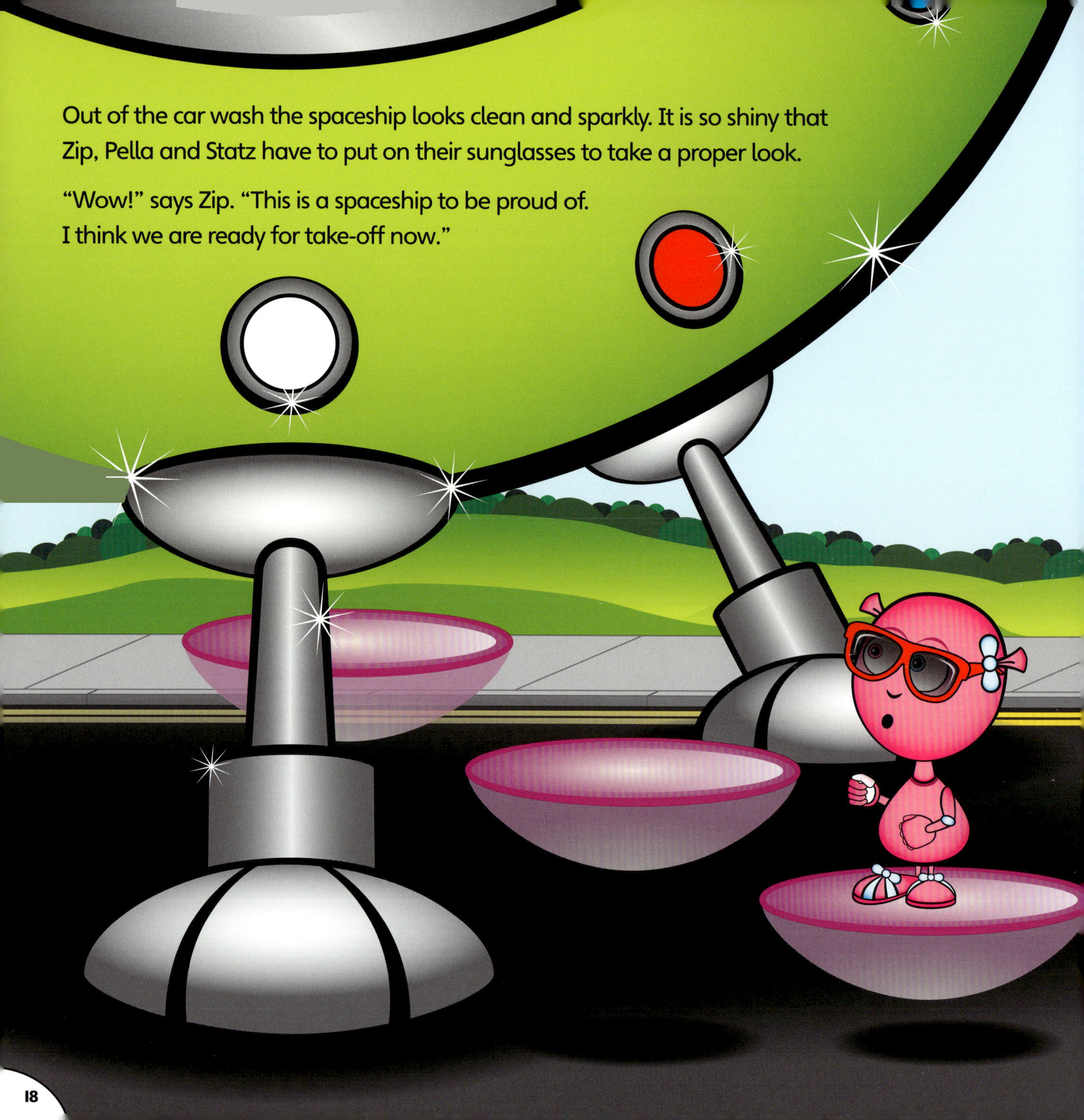

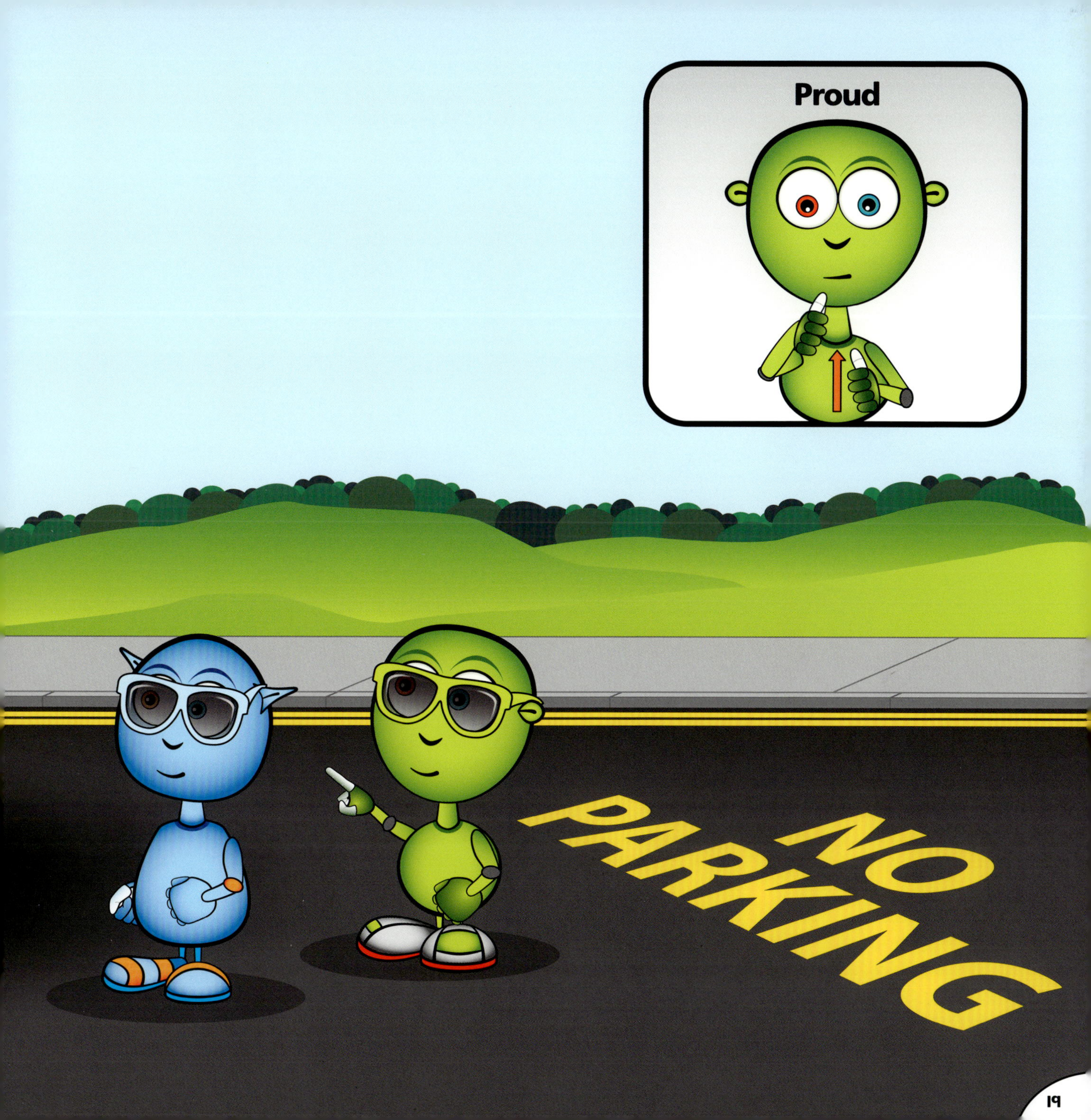
Proud
NO
PARKING

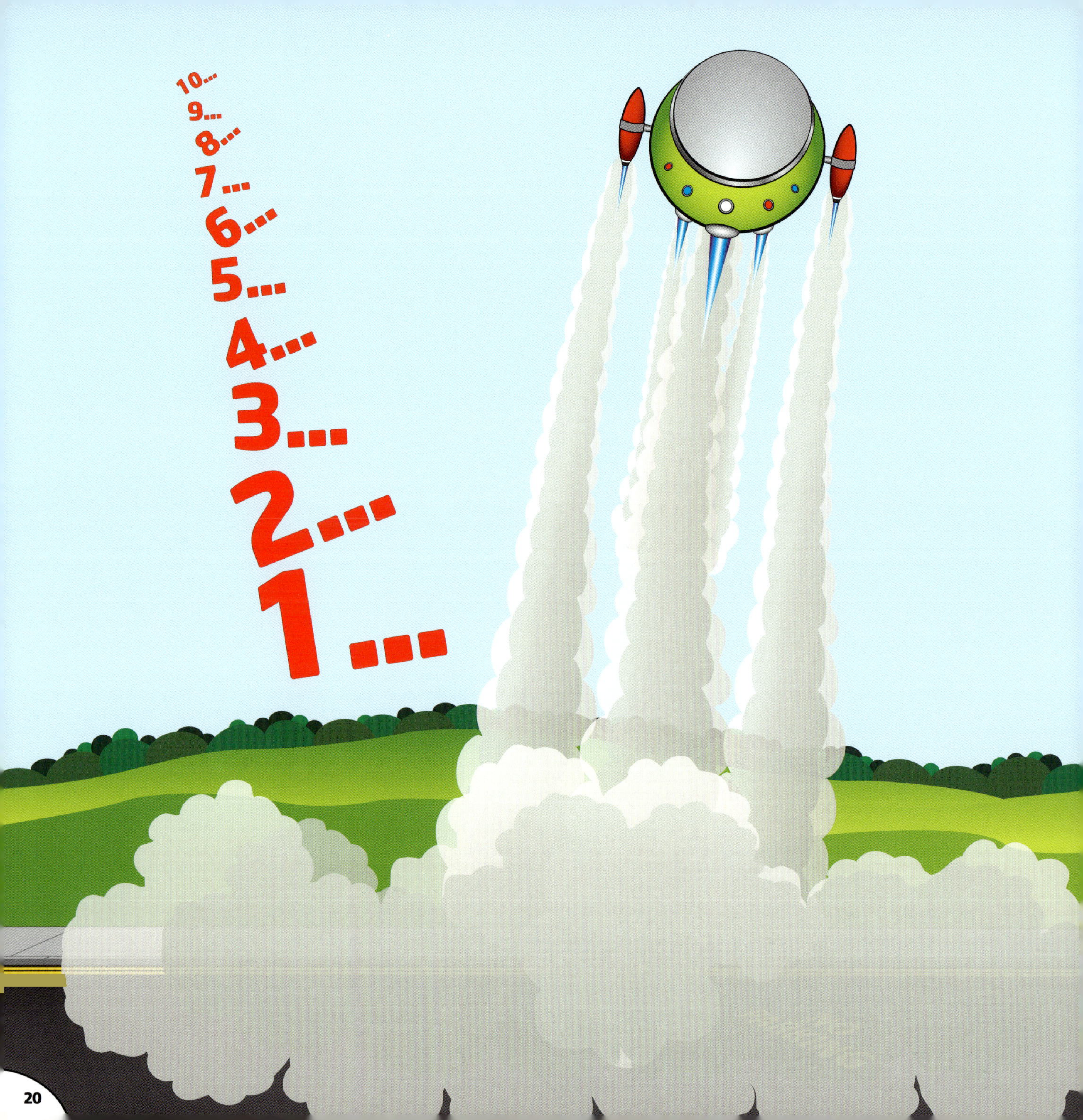
10...
9...
8...
7...
6...
5...
4...
3...
2...
1...

Zip, Pella and Statz are ready
for their journey home.
They are all very excited.
Statz counts down the launch.

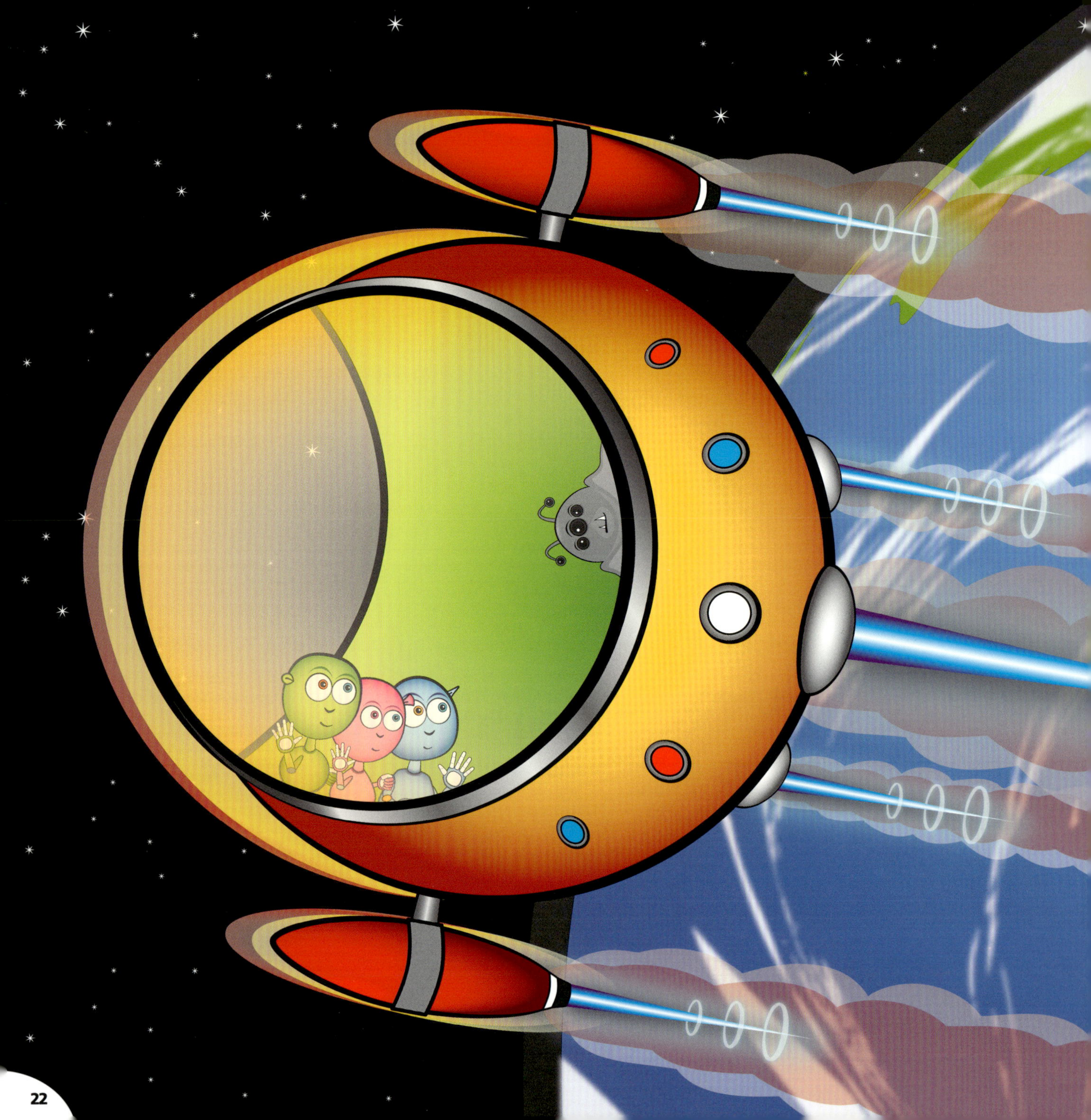

As the spaceship leaves the Earth's atmosphere, the friends wave goodbye. They are sad to be leaving, because they have had so many fun adventures.

Planet Earth becomes smaller and smaller as they whizz through space.

The friends happily settle into their journey knowing that they are on course and the computer will guide them home.

“Aaaawwwah,” yawns Statz. “I am going to go for a nap.”

Zip and Pella soon start to yawn too and follow Statz out of the control room to the sleep pod.
The lights turn off behind them.

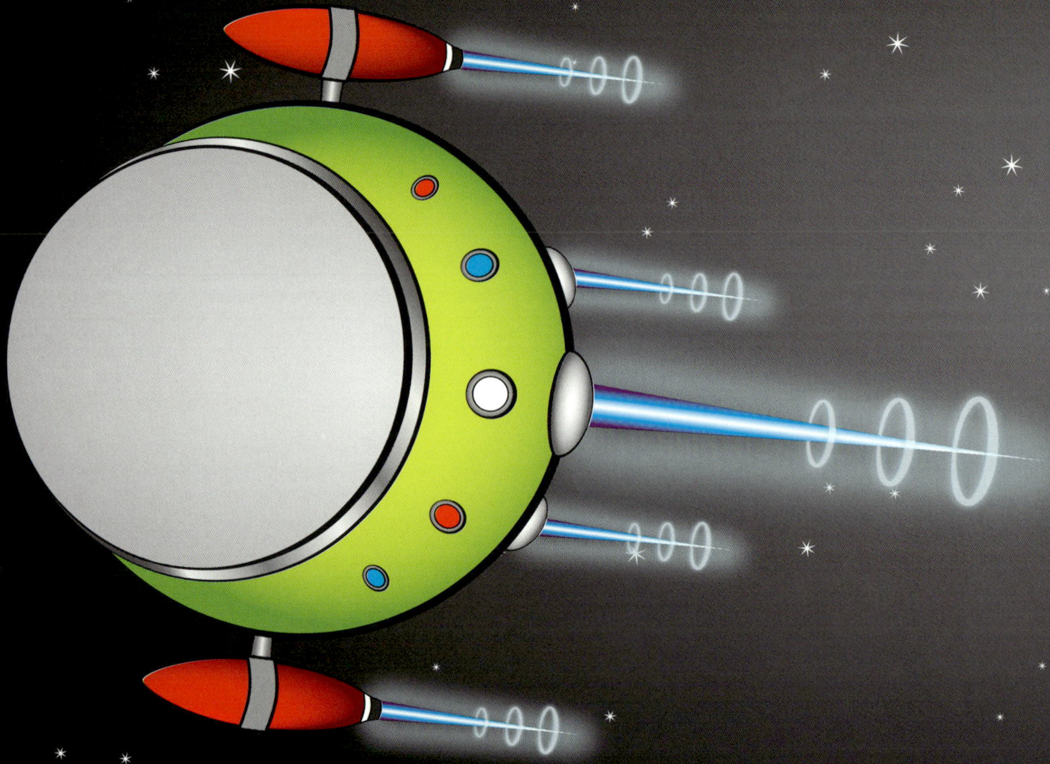

Space School

Take a look at the pictures below.
Can you remember the sign for how Zip is feeling?

Cross

Sad

Dislike

Excited

Proud

Embarrassed

Now the darkness of the control room is broken only by the soft red glow of the emergency button. It is a button that no one must ever press.

Something moves in the darkness.

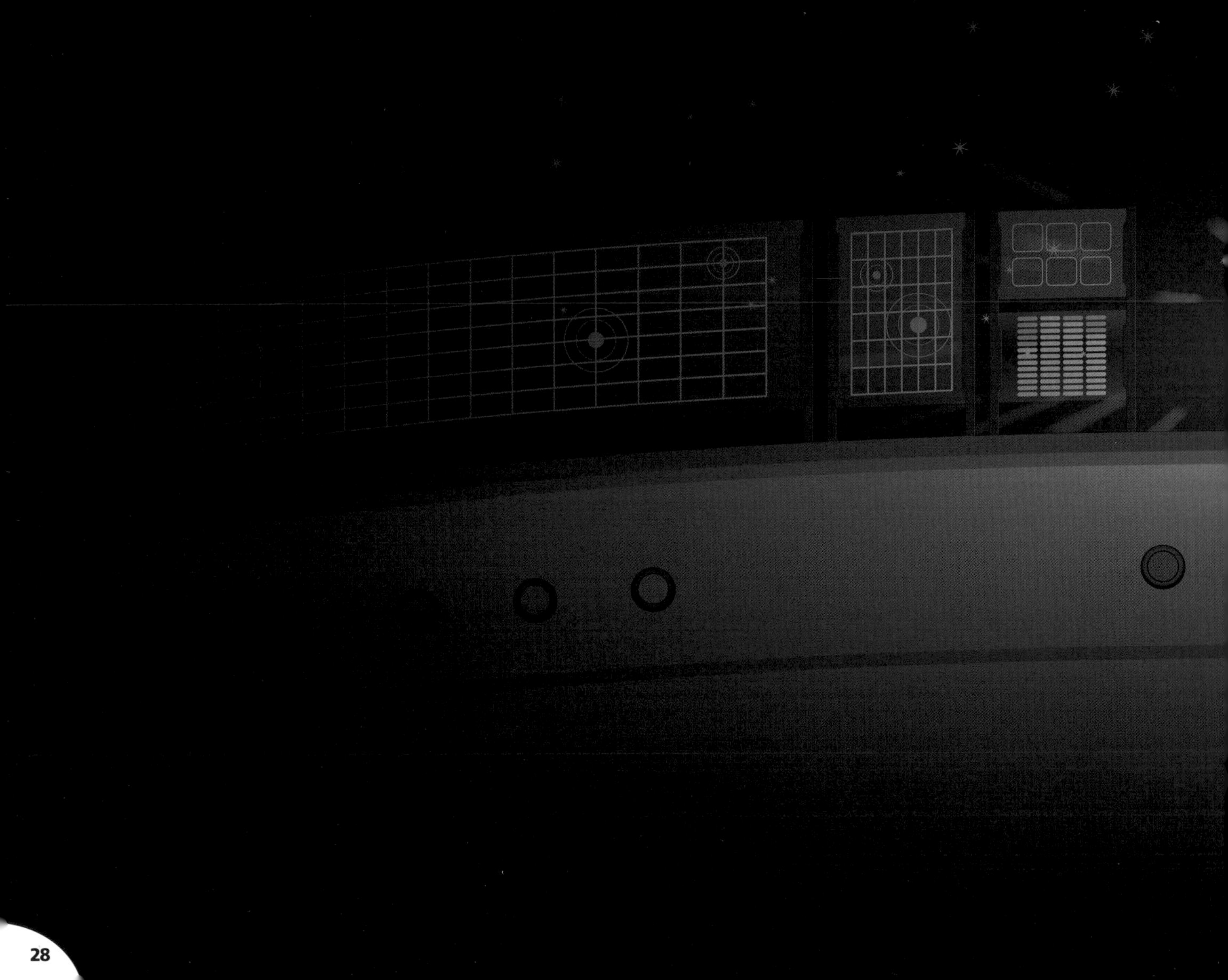

GOOBER!

Zip's Signs

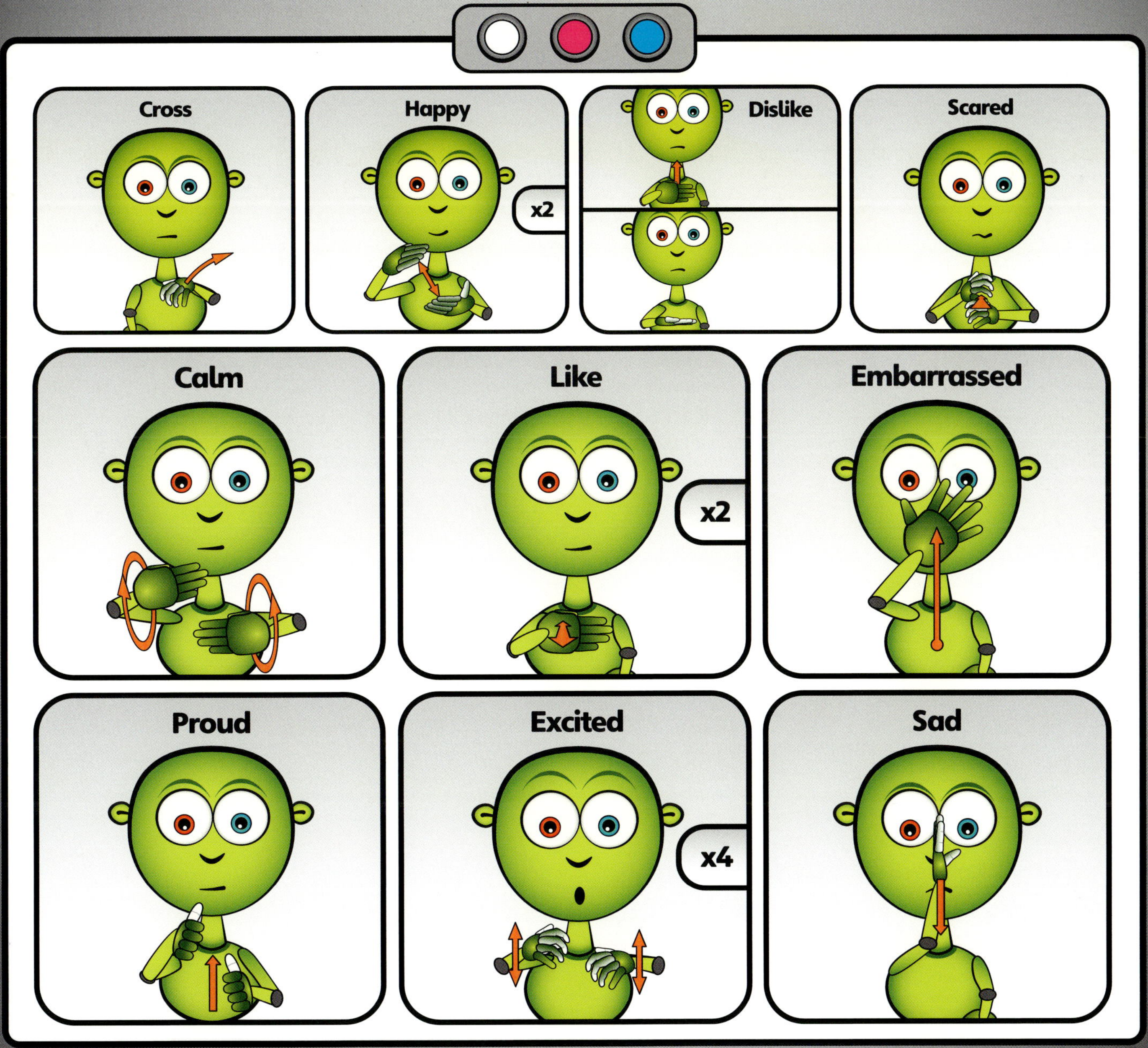
Cross
Happy
x2
Dislike
Scared
Calm
Like
x2
Embarrassed
Proud
Excited
x4
Sad

Fun things to do

Now that you have read all about Zip and the Journey Home, here are some fun things for you to do:

- **Create your own incoming message - describe, write or act**
- **If you were going on a long journey, what would you take with you?**
- **Who would you miss the most if you away from planet Earth for a long time?**
- **On planet Zee, how would Zip clean the spaceship?**
- **What do you think would happen if Goober pushed the red button?**
- **Teach a friend the sign for how you are feeling today**

First published 2013 by Signature

SignSpell® stories created by Signature
Designed and illustrated by Igloo Imaging Ltd.